MILK BLACK CARBON

PITT POETRY
PP
50
YEARS
SERIES

Ed Ochester, Editor

MILK

BLACK

CARBON

JOAN

NAVIYUK

KANE

UNIVERSITY OF PITTSBURGH PRESS

Published by the University of Pittsburgh Press, Pittsburgh, Pa., 15260

Copyright © 2017, Joan Naviyuk Kane

Manufactured in the United States of America

Printed on acid-free paper

10 9 8 7 6 5 4 3 2 1

ISBN 13: 978-0-8229-6451-3
ISBN 10: 0-8229-6451-1

Cover design by Joel W. Coggins

for the islanders, our island: qiġluiruŋa

CONTENTS

MILK BLACK CARBON

Iridin

A coastline, a transitional place
bears evidence of others dwelling:

a house pit in the shape of a nest,
another like a knife, a noose
not lost not in time. Ours

a useful relationship though not a tight one,
for between us we knew there was something to lose.

Fragrant in June heat & a field of confusion
nothing like metaphor: moss campion,
minute orchids, sweet

sweet vetch.

Salvage Phase

What he was the man could make
with little tools
                              assembled
devices   devastations

called by stone
                         saw and blade
back into the small study
of solder   wire
filament file and filigree

            destroy
rebuild
                    refine again

one's lungs fill with cold air
bone dust   a want
of space

livid hues   synthetic stone
encircles the neck
with rope with a wreath
            of rock

when I do not wish to
consider his hands
his money

plasticine discs
      in a chop uneven
draw along my collarbone

for what else learned
to hold me together?

At Bay

A metal roof thrashes in ceaseless gusts—
day is done, punctured. The stones
placed over the closed folds
of her eyes grow cold. The sea

a long line blurred forever
in the distance. Somewhere
snow falls on something illicit,
raising it into beauty:

a bramble of fresh hurt, its leaves
revived and green and again
incandescent with pollen.

Had she been able to step from the boat,
had she unloaded the small coffin—
had he received gifts at dawn,
hand-painted, mythical—

you'd funnel into this illusion,
your breath into the bellows.

All Night Long I Am Narrowing

I tried to pass safely through
danger, like you, the mate to a shoe
hurled by a breaking wave.

The sun never fell away.
It angled. I conjured
a small opening. How

a current drags out to sea
beyond a place you didn't pass,
but skirted. Perhaps not a current

but another woman. She tugs
the waves under, troubling the surface.
How often, who else? And what of.

Headline News

Compiled from *A History of the Alaskan Native as Published in the Headlines of the Nome Nugget from 1901 to 1976*

ESKIMOS HAVE VARIOUS THOUGHTS
ABOUT WOLVES.   FATHER TOM SAYS
ESKIMO LIFE DISTORTED BY CHEECHAKOS.

FOSTER WANTS TO KNOW WHO INTIMIDATED
NATIVES.   ESKIMO ENTERTAINMENT WELL
RECEIVED.   SCIENCE CONFIRMS ESKIMO

BELIEF ON POLAR BEAR LIVER.
DRUNKENNESS NAMED AS MAJOR PROBLEM
OF NATIVES.   HEALTH CONDITION OF

NATIVES UNFAVORABLE.   CLAIMS
ESKIMOS IN ALASKA HAVE BEEN BRAINWASHED.
NATIVES MAY TAKE POLAR BEAR FOR FOOD.

ALASKA ESKIMOS SAID TO HAVE RADIOACTIVITY.
BOTH ESKIMOS AND WHITES ARE SUBJECT
TO COLD WEATHER.   FAKE

ESKIMO ART.   ESKIMO BEAUTY QUEEN.
U. OF ALASKA MUSEUM ADDS ESKIMO
MARIONETTE. THREE ESKIMOS BURST

OUT OF SUBMERGED PLANE IN SELAWIK.
ESKIMOS TO GET ICE BOXES.   AN ENTIRE ESKIMO
VILLAGE MOVES FROM KING ISLAND TO NOME.

200 ESKIMOS DIE OF FLU.   ESKIMOS MEET AGAIN.
KING ISLAND ESKIMOS PUT ON PRE-HISTORIC
WOLF DANCE   FOR M-G-M.   ALASKA ESKIMO

SAYS SHE DOES NOT LIKE U.S.   ESKIMO ARTIST
PAINTS LIFE THE WAY IT WAS IN DAYS GONE BY.
ESKIMO GIRL WANTS ASSAILANT'S SCALP.

NATIVE GIRL SUICIDES ON PUBLIC STREET.

ESKIMOS VISUALIZE HELL AS FINE PLACE TO LIVE.

An Other Lethe

The drag hook of the mind asthenic
catches yet on green not so gone
though scrolled in absent a horizon
banked with clouds turning forth,

driven by wind. Let us set nostalgia
in a harness. A pathogen is drawn
upstream from metal culvert buckled
in sweet brook water underroad again.

Let us see dust risen into light, subtracted
into rain. Our spring runs dry beneath
snow on a land now arid, now seam
of admonition: do not solve, adapt.

Incognitum (in the Indian Hall)

At Monticello the skeletons assemble,
buried trade beads brought to light
gleam like ruin run glamorous alluvium:

evidence of someone else's way through valleys
dense, interior and distant. I want for hands
in ocher, for one whose hands once held my own.

I learn to long for thought arising through the floor
of my mind, a song alone in sound
recessed into the small noise of my breath.

The tongue turns—
        It may be asked, why I insert
     the mammoth, as if
        it still existed? I ask in return
   why I should omit . . .

I am little more than a string figure, one
of a divided couple danced into a seam of time.
At the margin of such desolation a relic so worn

bears no odor.
      He may well exist there now,
        as he did formerly where we find his bones.
The eye of a storm stares inward:

all fallen together, yours for excavation.

Exhibits from the Dark Museum

In a shop of bloat and blown glass,
I pry an iridescent green beetle alive
from my ear and chase a dwindled trail

paved dire with coins towards three skulls
enclosed in a box of Olympia beer. Pale
grass: vitiligo thrust from the tract

of his scalp, now mine. Your voice,
a sforzando of light as it strikes the rock-
ridge hung above the dwellings.

Or, your voice, a grim notation of the sweep
between us. All night along with you
our sons respire. I fever through memory.

The world that survives me but a dangerous place.

Inuŋuaq

Uniplaaguruq samma suli:
pigitpaktaqtut aġnat,
sawitpaaqtut.

Aŋutitun sayuapaaqtuq aġnaq.
Aŋutitun ilipłuni, sayuapaaqtuq aŋutitun.
Suŋuaqtuanigliqaa piraqtut.

Iuqpaktuk aqqataani.
Iuqpaktua.
Tavra kannuzukaluaqłuŋa tauq,

isaaq imam qaŋasaq.

The Dolls

There is another old story:
the women's bodies were bent in toil,
they worked very hard.

A woman would dance very hard like a man.
Acting like men, they would strut like men.
They pretended to be whatever we could conceive.

Ice pressure ridges were forming all around us.
Pressure ridges were building with great intensity.
I felt quite shy about it too,

from times long ago, beyond memory.

Vanishing Point

He fixed in my heart
the small hard pebble—
we speak a language
with no one else.

Wheel of the old thing
thrown out makes a cold
circuit. Three nights
ago an apparition

urged me to repent.
The city is his, it glisters.
I worried snow down
from the roof. It buried me.

A grid of lights gave way
to another body, thin relief
of land beneath
too little snow and no—

I have watched other
women twist their locks
into gleam and gloss
and have swallowed

a battery, passel, past.

Give or Take a Century

A man goes on a journey, a woman does not.
Instead, birches murmur into the song
of a bird unseen, the forest endlessly receding.

To be alone and without purpose: a seed
borne on wind to flat stones arrayed
on the remote shore. Witness to news,

songs, myelin. One of our last
a succession of ribs distinct and vast
in sudden collapse. Mother, we make

no choices. Mother, he counts our frail bones.

Late Successional

You ask

to lead me to me
to lead you next

to colors all wet:
bark saturated brown,
brown-green

      where lichen scurries up the trunk
of a tree that needs it.

You make me wonder about thirst,
the way things work together.
Boughs once empty fill with birds

in rapid flickering flight until beat, wingbeat,
winged threat: a magpie I try to wish away.

I ask, do not disappear.
That is no kind of apology
and I have never been a forgiver.

The green part of me never leaves
however I find that it remains with you.
However I find it in you

you must remember I am not a soft woman.
You'll seek the mother in me

but expect to see splinters,
rolled margins.

Together we have never been so alone,
like ladders, like messengers with another
answer. The ink-stained hand holds

heartache no longer. It's been set
and pressed down, mapped & scattered.

Epithalamia

Butane, propane
and lungfull of diesel.
I did not stand a chance.

Always with poison
breath, bill, responsibility.
A man with rote hands.

Everything in exchange,
rain in a frozen season.
Our roof, roofs strung

with hot wire. Our love,
what was, an impression
of light, gaunt: there is

nothing to get.

Taktugziun

Manimaiga—
maliŋniagratugut
mallatuq.

Nuyaqtuŋa. Taqqiq,
ikpiŋanailaq,
iluilaq.

Ilisiruŋa, ilita.tuŋa.
Ilaiyairuŋa akłunaamiik.
Qaaġaaŋa.

Uaałukitaaqtuq umiaq.
Quliaqtuŋa aptauqtuaŋa—
iitaaga pularuq.

ilaŋa.tuq.

Compass

I let him do what he will to me—
we are traveling into the waves
and the ocean is torn by swells.

I am cautious. The moon,
it can barely be sensed,
it cannot be helped.

I learned something, I am learning.
I am untangling a rope.
I am caught by a breaking wave.

The boat is rolling from side to side
I tell of my going to town—
what he threw broke through,

it has broken away.

The Incident Light

I went for relief
of the mind, to move
into currents of worry.

I did not know
what the body held.

I thought I would turn
through broken ice
and disappear
                    the features
of apprehension, of influence.

If only I could betray
the brute matter.

If only the seas had
not erased the facture,
ladder, the easy reach.

Instead we sank
into soft snow,

four women ascending
together the deep furrow
worn by water
returning to water:

Ayagaduk, Uyuguluk,
Yaayuk, Naviyuk.

I was startled, at once
aware that the far road
had fractured, done
under by the fault
we fought to bury.

Land arises
beyond a treble
of strong currents.

The boat that bears
us rises in them.

With invisible stars
we share blood.

Those seas, increased,
might scour and reflect—
those seas, increased,

rephrase us.

In Its Mouth

Mottled gray and gold
through alders dense—

like a wreath, scapular,
her garland of reversal.

A garment corners the woman
I was to have become, whose

hipbone juts just so, traced
and splayed like brambles bent

to a wooden floor.
Bone unfurled, unfurling.

Sea as heavy as pencil lead,
ice from shore to shore as leads

draw together, subsuming
something smudged out.

Glassy as seal oil. Surface
hoar collapses, collapsing.

Imaaġruk
only a word between us.

Little Air

A tress or tree, one or the other
fell when he blew his breath—
then rain, its wind, came closing in
through a hole in the roof

where humankind would never
be nurtured. I give no opposition
to the sky, I will leave
                              no stone ring

behind beyond the outer
walls where my abolished house
once stood, as it stands now,
open to magpies strayed too late

into a thin season, their noise
mistaken for a complicated engine.

A Few Lines for Jordin Tootoo

> When I was drinking, I was selfish because of my addiction
> to popularity and being out in the public eye. I used that as
> a mechanism to create commotion with everyone. And if I
> got into trouble away from the rink, I made it up on the ice.
>
> —*Jordin Tootoo*

What do you see out there on the ice?
Perhaps something dark, far off,
louder than the bellowing headlines
in the otherwise technical silence.

In a lecture hall, once, in Barrow,
I listened while the ice of the Beaufort Sea
split into blue leads three months early.
What I heard was: if only we learned

the old ways, we'd learn where we fit
in life, how critical we are to each other.
That a hunt done right results in little
suffering or loss. That the migrations

of fowl, fish, and mammals will continue.
What I wanted to hear was a reassurance.
Some kind of premonition or promise:
when words come back, so do the other things

or *words come back when you have a chance
to learn them.* Instead, what I hold within
is the felt absence of place. A land of great
failure, abundance: it goes on without us.

Another time up north, maybe by mistake,
I was invited to watch the men butchering
but I didn't want to see where it was
they found the heart, if they ever did.

Like you, in front of me is all I have.
In the distance, mostly, another world.

Update on J

She is beset by the recurrent burial of women
in grounds profane and consecrated.

If now amid crag and tundra, she would mull
the vapors of starry cassiope and smooth cliff fern.

Instead, a must of high swamp with its admirable
bolete, stream violet, green spleenwort.

Concerning her parents she is nostalgic.
Concerning another she is silent.

She would wish her arms and the arms
of her children to be fortunate.

On no day does she not comprehend
what is forbidden to her: a refusal of some

prohibitions. For instance, one must not consume
or traffic in lupine. Moved by conspicuous vice

she made confession and received the sacrament.
As well as she could you can see how she fared.

It is true that she wishes for a voice
to aid self-governance: though obedient

in many things we now find her color high
and too easily touched to the quick.

She did her best to conceal all intrigue
as she feared most your treacheries.

She has unlearned *A* from *B*. She knows little
of belief, less of being believed.

Held back from accomplishment,
she grows ill-content.

On a journey away she meets no hindrance
save a discontinuous thicket of alders

and anxieties before a semantic freedom
to be used fruitfully. She denies

that she has been failed. After all,
there is light all about.

The things she has done are not in despair but . . .

Language transforms her thoughts.
Thought, apprehensible to the senses.

Tomorrow she will not go out.
Tonight let us let her.

Glare in Blue

I was not lost without you,
only torn from myself:

a lake lapsed back into the soil
and innocent of assent.

In a house constructed of mud
the walls would not answer.

Removed in the wrong direction
from a winter storm

created distantly, and landed,
I would have worn a dark hand

to see you, root, made fast
at my margin. As the clouds

with their many shapes
draw across the sky,

we are the both of us buried.

When the World Was Milk

Seized between breaths the hard mother of the brain—
twice pierced through, atremble too with the anesthetist's
imprecision. I

could not walk for days
but fed, or tried to feed, shuffling flowers
stiff and white and dry as paper

for I could not lift a pitcher to refill
the water drawn out beneath them.
Men surround me, or will, all yellow

sclera, thunder, & fallow.

Song

I made a song in thirds and two remain, ravined,
while seasonally the gully swells with sound.

On the ground we twine grass,
plait it thickly, its odor in the sun
dissolves with the salt

of the sea, forever rising.

The man who breaks bones makes a song
while winds strew pebbles aloft
and carry clouds away.

Across a rock slide his trail
scales steep towards three tiers
of willow leaves barren

of caribou, gone to feed.

It is said that far beyond Imuruk Basin
huge birds hunt whales on the open ocean.

Once shoved downslope by downbeat gusts
the man alone fell to one knee, erred, aimed
and pierced such a bird between its breast

and the narrow column of its neck. Careening

first up into the air then a swaying slip
into the valley below

                              it's come to rest
beyond the subterranean terminus

of a rivulet sourced from snow on snow.

Assiraġia

Taalutabluu
                    ialiq.
Nalunaqtuq.

Sillaga
tammaighiga.
uniplaaguruq samma suli—

nalliġaġlau.
Ganuqtun itpa?

I Am Copying Him

Drag the dark
                into the room.
I have something to confess.

My heaven
I cannot find it.
Just another old story—

let me pay for it.
How much is it?

Point Transience

Under winter and below a hill of thin blue clay
the waves were high and rising, water
turning back, folding over and opening

into an ebb more precise than absent—
The hood of his coat a distant bloom
when she began to weep for him,

his sled trace a sulcus hard and frozen in.

For her I sought and gathered wood—
dry willow twigs, a jettisoned mast,
sticks staged for hanging damp packs

of garments to take notice of the wind—

Let us plait our smoke thick into the pitched sky.

Human Heart Toponymic

No privacy in the north of me,
the place where ice piles up,
altogether too contracted
for distance of the social kind.

Between the squalor of my love
and intruders emplaced, how again
and over again I've lost my way,
ignorant of the names of places.

A shame to ask anyone to guide me,
gone through a valley in which I forget
currents of air as they course between slopes.
The breath stops in my chest—

there is way I have of holding on to it
as it splits me into something more.
A stack of stones uneven, the mind
fixing customs from origins. I find

no processional line. Instead
it is as if I were to become human
through a series of transformations.
Thus, as directed by my mother, I culled

small rocks but found them, in the end,
to be a strand of beads, the hole in each
growing smaller. Merestones, my one:
let us name them together.

Savak Aŋmaiga / I Opened the Door

The fictions of an eternal blue noon,
small throes of women in the engine
whose green tresses noiselessly tangle
into *Artemisia tilesii* as if bruised underfoot—

where he pelts the shadow cast down
upon a thin layer of new ice, never dry,
upon hollow bed of waters run again
into the notion of a distant silver chord.

I don't advance a step. The mind, too—
erratic, distracted, is discontinuous at best.

Earnings Statement

She is not
as she used to be,
the bird with the bit in her beak.

Note the void, not oblivion:

a tightness of mind.

Last season a white spruce

spilt in strong wind,

its boughs downed
around its stump.

A torn thing

survived by the flushed

fruit of the sour drupe

clustered beneath it.

Cramp bark, viburnum,
misnomer. A darkblack

cloud
above open water

if our weather is apt to vary.

The woman
drifted in deep with words

finds inferior comfort

all over hell,

her ancient region.

Georgic

Not a fume of bird,
but syrinx enough to fill
the friable air with thin song
and batter rime down in switches.

These too are statistic,
favored by chance— alit
on a chain link fence, made divisible
into wildernesses peculiar.

Our mouths muttered
with charcoal, paintball:
let us together find the end
of this and every other settlement.

Peripheral Vision

It is not winedark. Its bright break a page of script repeating—
there is not land and land submerged. Everyone sleeps.

Let us return to chase the thoughts the waves erase
and rake over again in a mind following the heat of its fevers—

the woods gone white. Winter of a prime disturbance,
said before, subsumed, and said again.

Hours until the sun cusps the brow of the mountains
that ring the wolves away. A hush peculiar from months of rain

and wind lifting the eaves, rindling rot and gape. Child,
I am called to carry you to see the world, snowy as it was

before, but more so, and so still, with other snow yet overhead.

Stemmata

One I will have nothing to do with,
American in all her lineages.
I know what she will say—

find me something frail
in a gloss of day

on the black branches
of the white birches.

She only knows the trees
by the scent of their shoots
when the ground is hot—

but I know, you know,
of other stars in cold
and disappearing places.

The Straits

Ledum, Labrador Tea, *saayumik*.
A matted growth beneath the most shallow
depth of snow on record in all our winters.

Pausing upbluff from the edge of ice
I broke from branches leaves to pin
between my teeth and tongue

until warmed enough for their fragrant
oil to cleanse you from me.

Somewhere in a bank of fog
beyond the visible end of open water,
alleged hills were windfeathered—

drainages venous. In routes
along the shore forever slipping
under, I am reminded — in the city

one finds it simple to conceive nothing
but a system, and nothing but a world of men.

Held

Nalausrivik: one
      drove the caribou into the lake
to kill them, below the weak ice
      water billowing underfoot.

Light insufficient, dim and artificial,
I twist my legs beneath me behind a desk.
Sawittuŋa: at least I am trying to work
although

      yes, *uiqaatuŋa*:
I do have a husband.

Suksraniaqpin? The inquest boiled
up the bluff and back down again.

Wolves, I answered. *Amaġut
qiniqsuitkiga*, I was always watching
for wolves.

The Mother of All

Skies above the thicket set aflame north of here.
Our metropolis a crowd spawned-out.

Black cottonwood limbs frame the strath
hung already with snow.

A small room choked with fatty smoke threw
a glint so slight as to redouble the dark
between the peaks, between them
or us, intricate and muddled.

At every sound I was undone,
demolished, diminished.

You dreamt I walked once,
across the ice, to find you.
It was moving always. I,
a girl disappeared,
not carnelian propelled
forth: but waste wax
and fine wire. And so we were
bound together. Elsewhere

wind moves through
the crowns of trees

beyond a window, like weather
impends over some ocean
infixed within. I am not there

and never was. Together,
perhaps, we will fare.
Or you will go & I will follow,
sinew stitched through skin

on skin—as you do not hesitate,
but decide when to set in motion
and then keep moving. The crab
who loves her lure is kept on,

hoisted, after her line's been
lifted through seawater
scooped clear of slush ice
as it forms: frazil in a current

of constant movement
against the stiff disbelief

that ice cannot issue from
the depths of this or any other sea.

As if suddenly I
imagine the boards
burnt if boards remain.

My firstborn asserts:
these are lines, this is sound
& this is the speaker.

Until we come to a stand
of tall grass with long roots
in loose sand, I leave aside
interpretation, remission
and removal.

A horizon of blue-white silk,
a wide snow-scoured contoured
hillside thick with thoughts

tugged & stuck
in a scrub of willows.

How time passes just as the light
does: it darkens and is gone.

Ugiuvak

Elsewhere ice is forming on rocks along the shore:
our sky awash from one ink to white.

Another daughter I will not have will not get there.

She will never gather wood for whittling
nor noose rabbits. Along with the brother
I live without, his unknown treachery.

Roots remain ungathered, points of navigation
resolve to nothing, arbitrary.

More Dissipate

We strove to locate love on a list of symptoms
hyaline when held to light and found instead
nothing but bones, and of the sort you relish:

a kind of bicker in the throat. A jetblack end.
We thought we saw the dark cursive of a wolf
circling on sea ice, miles out, in an hour

not blue, though persuasive and brief.
In looking back, it was not dog. It wasn't
anything. It was not the heart burst forth

but another part: one for which the words,
the shafts and shanks, their shifts, have long
been sung, and in the same breath, lost.

Bone Mineral

Ruse a flame back into being for ice that doesn't appear
to move. Transform into an owl arising away
and do not turn back.

With it cold enough yet for the sun to be missed,
scrape the pitch to mend the rifts in the hull of the boat
split during rough portage. Will we return together

beyond the blue white churn of the ocean, so vast,
at the jut of rock? There must have been known
to us alone a line, a brink, a bluff long private.

One could not cross the shoals or trouble surfaces
left worse without reversion from *I did not know,*
but now I know you. A life thick with pieces moving

with concision: a hell of lexical squall. Some do not deal
with loss, but provision and build, eye and embody.
Her sky above the horizon, her stone and pewter light—

row upon row of peaks like teeth, like winter furrows,
snares of white. The improbable order of ash and snow
falling back to fill the emptied sky: a blue bead I bury

to mark our quarrel, its profusion, and its sea of milk.

The Unnamed Child

Supplicants, or soul and string:
a battery of trees bound fast,
askance. We stretched the sinew

from tangled roots of coarse grass.
Another time she will reach
the goal she now gives up.

Let her look the father in the face.
The moon would be his head:
it thinks, she thought, for no one.

A Wall Collapsed

Like light within linen,
its movement in a small field.
Harmless and visible,
its brilliance a sheen—

a river swayed out in depth
uncluttered by sediment.
I found a silver way to the sea.
Scree and scission tighten

the ligaments rigged to the hollow
behind my knee— should I
be troubled by the land,
locked, let me know the pass

through which I must travel,
composed again—

Up the Mountain

Cover him with willows to spare him
the ravage of wind.

It brought a carrion bird bound from oxbow
to the bend of the cove in which we found no shelter,
no firmament, no family, no flicker of light.

Azure beyond fissure of shore ice and ocean,
the current a warm river once under, not open.

Aspirational Phase

One desert summer a girl fed to fatten mice,
all trisomy and bled quickly. Little obliterations.
With scalpel and solution she fixed the discs of eyes
to slides for study. Another way to see the world,
it was: smog, wistfulness & sprinkler hiss each night,
all night, until the morning sprawl beneath palms
and the bell-tower tolling

        go back, go back,
go forward

Arboretum Americanum

"The animals go extinct in zoos," my younger son
says to me one afternoon as I grade and fuss.
Birch leaves filter light into his green truth.

Last year's tall grass was not lost to snow:
it pales still, turning and nodding, ready to burn
thick at the base of black spruce whose gnarled

boles tilt as the ground beneath them slumps
and gives in fine spring heat come two months
too soon. His older brother, just eight, cuts

second molars into gums that redden and strain.
Unfamiliar limbs lengthen into long bones
as he strides away. Geese and gulls war

a garrulous roof overhead, filling as flocks
would the sky with finish and divergence. A boy
I considered a man and also, once, a friend,

and a woman who could have never once
been gentle enough to be a girl are the birds
that don't come back, the birds that never were.

Perhaps I ask them, "What is it you wanted me
to be sad about?" Perhaps the boots that are split,
I cannot mend them now—a nib drifts like the needle

in a compass. Perceive the gales as they rage beyond
far tracts of red yew, which fracture and split
under the weight of late growth. We overact.

I am of disproportionate weakness. The domes
submerged, like the old stories, like dreams—
I cannot hold them in my head.

Metabole

In song, swamp has another name.
There source countless ways
to say we yet lack snow to sound.

I would not form the words
with softer syntax: a bone skewer
must close the bag of broth

from a seal whose body must never
know your ammunition. I lost
my breath in strands that gave

rise to winds, in summer
and your other kind of abundance.
May we find a swell upon the ocean

and never long to leave it
and make our minds together
fresh and green as deep sea weeds.

Hearth He Burnt

Our daughter uncoils from the course
       mistaken— let, let

us position her well even as the tern banks,
       banked, and moves on.

She perceives,   far off, my body still
body as it comes into glass,

breaking it. Until we release her
       her name,

we will not be retained in this song.

To Live Beyond

She is said to carry a wooden box
instead of a basket, the one who appears
when you lay to waste while others
would never capitulate—

you vanish into another kind
of silence or the sky a constant blue,

you return from the end of the plain
between the shins of peaks you have yet
to gain, to gather water, water, splendor.

ACKNOWLEDGMENTS

Grateful acknowledgement is made to the editors of the following, in which versions of these poems have appeared:

    Alaska Quarterly Review: "A Wall Collapsed," "Little Air," "Stemmata," "The Straits," "Exhibits from the Dark Museum," "Metabole," "Point Transience," "Nine Lines Against Dreamless Sleep"; *American Poets Magazine*: "Taktugziun | Compass"; *Best American Poetry*: "Exhibits from the Dark Museum"; *Boston Review*: "Late Successional," "Aspirational Study," "Iridin"; *Broadsided Press*: "Inuŋuaq | The Dolls"; *Columbia Magazine*: "Song"; *Ghost Town*: "Up the Mountain, " "Bone Mineral," "Salvage Phase," "Peripheral Vision"; *Hick Poetics*: "The Mother of All," "Catalytic," "Human Heart Toponymic," "At Bay"; *Kin Poetry Journal*: "To Live Beyond"; *The Mind of Monticello: 50 Contemporary Poets on Jefferson*: "Incognitum"; *NAT. BRUT*: "HEADLINE NEWS," "Ugiuvak"; *POETRY*: "Epithalamia"; *Prairie Schooner*: "A Few Lines for Jordin Tootoo"; *Taos Journal*: "Assiraġia | I Am Copying Him"; *West Branch*: "When the World Was Milk," "Held."

With thanks to Alaska Pacific University, the Alaska State Council on the Arts, the Alaska Arts and Cultures Foundation, the Anchorage Museum's Polar Lab, the Hurford Center for the Humanities at Haverford College, the International Writing Program's Reading Abroad: American Writers on Tour initiative, the Rasmuson Foundation, the School for Advanced Research, and the Woodland Pattern Book Center for the resources of time and space to write these poems. Much appreciation for Voices from the American Land/Center for the Study of Place for the opportunity to work on *The Straits*.

All gratitude to my family and to my colleagues and students in the low-residency MFA program in creative writing at the Institute of American Indian Arts.